my
SIKH
FAITH

About this book

The titles in the *My Faith* collection are designed to introduce
faiths and each focuses on a child and his or her family from
Whilst the approach and the language level are appropriat
key concepts will need to be supported by sensitive clarificc
Teachers and Parents on pages 4 and 5 provide extra inforn
knowledge and understanding of the different beliefs and t

First published in this edition in 2006 by
Evans Brothers Limited
2A Portman Mansions
Chiltern St
London W1U 6NR

Printed in China by WKT Company Limited

British Library Cataloguing in Publication Data

Singh, Kawal
    My Sikh faith. - (My Faith)
    1. Sikhism - Juvenile literature
    I. Title II. Knott, Lynda
    051999
    ISBN 023753230 1
    13 digit ISBN (from 1 January 2007) 9780237 53230 7

Editor: Su Swallow
Design: D.R. ink
Production: Jenny Mulvanny
Reading consultant: Lesley Clark, Reading and Language Information Centre
Series consultant: Alison Seaman, The National Society's Religious Education Centre
Photography: Vip Rao

Acknowledgements
The author and publishers would like to thank Simran Singh and his family for their help in making this
book.
©Evans Brothers Limited 1999

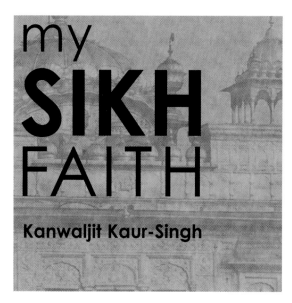

my SIKH FAITH

Kanwaljit Kaur-Singh

Contents

Evans

Notes for Teachers and Parents

Pages 6/7 Sikhism was started by Guru Nanak who was born in Punjab in India in 1469 CE and gave his first sermon at about the age of 30 years. Guru Nanak established the system of Guruship and was followed by nine Gurus. Guru Gobind Singh, the tenth Guru, ended the line of Gurus and gave Guruship to the Sikh holy book, the Guru Granth Sahib. The Sikhs believe that Gurus were special people chosen and inspired by God to give God's message to people. The Sikh Gurus taught that everyone has the right to choose their way of life, and defending the weak is a sacred duty of every Sikh. The majority of Sikh names can be used for boys and girls. A girl's name is followed by 'Kaur' and a boy's name by 'Singh'. So you might meet a boy called Simran Singh and a girl called Simran Kaur. Kaur means princess and Singh means lion. The Sikhs believe that there is only one God. The symbol in the picture is Ik Onkar, meaning one God.

Pages 8/9 Sikhs believe that there is only one God and the whole universe is created by one and the same God, who is omnipresent. The whole of humanity is equal in God's eyes. There is no one inferior or superior because of his or her birth. All people rich or poor, black or white, Christians, Jews, Muslims, Hindus or Sikhs are equal to God. God does not make any distinction between religions. It is the actions of people that make them good or bad.

Pages 10/11 A gurdwara is a place of Sikh worship, where the Sikh holy book, the Guru Granth Sahib is kept. Every gurdwara has the Sikh flag, the Nishan Sahib, flying outside it. In the middle of the flag is the Khanda, the Sikh symbol, depicted in the border. The Khanda represents justice and freedom. Around the Khanda is a circle called a Chakra which reminds Sikhs of God's infinite power. On the outside of the Khanda are two kirpans (swords) which remind Sikhs of their spiritual and secular responsibilities. The gurdwaras usually have a prayer hall, dining hall, rooms for classes to teach Panjabi and music. Gurdwaras are run by management committees chosen by the congregation. Most Sikhs have a prayer room at their homes where they keep the Guru Granth Sahib. That room is also called a gurdwara.

Pages 12/13 The Sikhs believe that the Gurus were God-inspired, and their writings revealed God's message, which are collected in the Guru Granth Sahib. The Guru Granth Sahib is written in poetry and is set to ragas (musical notations) for singing, and is written in Panjabi. The writing is referred to as shabads (hymns).

Pages 14/15 Sikh men and women do not cut their hair, it is part of the five Ks, which forms the Sikh uniform. Because of their uncut hair which grows long, the Sikh boys are sometimes addressed as girls and can fall prey to teasing and bullying. Teachers and parents need to be sensitive to this issue. Sikh men who practise their religion can easily be recognised by their turbans and beards. Young girls wear their hair loose or plait it and women tie it in a knot at the back of their neck.

Pages 16/17 Everyone who visits the gurdwara shows their respect by removing shoes, covering their heads and bowing before the Guru Granth Sahib, before sitting down to listen to shabads. In this country, men and women sit on separate sides. It is a social custom and not a religious edict.

Pages 18/19 In Sikhism there is no priestly class. Any man or woman who can read the Guru Granth Sahib can conduct the services and perform all the ceremonies, but often it is read by an appointed 'granthi' (literally maning a reader of Guru Granth Sahib). Similarly whoever can sing, can take part in singing the shabads during the services and ceremonies. However, many gurdwaras employ professional singers called ragis, as it is difficult to rely on volunteers. Sikhism believes that religions are different paths leading to the same God, therefore anyone who wants to worship can join without any distinction of gender, colour, creed or status.

Pages 20/21 The langar is the name for the food and the dining hall of a gurdwara. All people who attend a service are expected to stay afterwards to eat together. This is a reminder that all people belong to the same family of God and should be treated equally. Volunteers (both men and women) from the community cook and serve food, which is always vegetarian, so that everyone is able to eat.

Pages 22/23 In the Gurdwara, classes are held to teach Panjabi and to play the musical instruments, the drums and the harmonium. These classes are held on Saturdays or Sundays so that children can attend easily without disrupting their main schooling. The Sikhs believe that it is important for children to learn to read Panjabi so that they can read the Guru Granth Sahib. Sikhs lay great importance in family life. Looking after and teaching their children the Sikh way of life is very important. Therefore, the adults in the extended family, whenever they visit, take an opportunity to teach children the teachings contained in the Guru Granth Sahib, and stories of the Gurus' and other Sikhs' lives.

Page 24 The five Ks are: the Kes, uncut hair, a sign of saintliness; Kanga, a comb, it represents cleanliness; Kacch (shorts), a symbol of sexual purity and self-restraint; Kara, a steel bangle, it reminds Sikhs to always do the right thing; Kirpan, a sword, a symbol to remind Sikhs to defend the weak. Wearing these five symbols reminds Sikhs to live according to the Gurus' teachings.

Pages 25/26 Sikh festivals are called gurpurab, meaning the Guru's day. In this country the Sikhs celebrate their festivals on weekends. Sikhs celebrate the festival of Vaisakhi with great enthusiasm. This was the day when Guru Gobind Singh tested his Sikhs to see if they were ready to follow the Sikh teachings. With a sword in hand he asked for a Sikh to come forward who was willing to give his life for God and Guru. In total, the Guru asked for five Sikhs. He called the first five who came forward the panj piarey (five beloved ones) and gave them amrit (the Sikh initiation) and asked them to wear the five Ks. Five Sikhs representing the panj piarey take part in major celebrations. Panj piarey head the major celebrations for Sikh festivals.

Page 27/28 Other major Sikh festivals are Guru Nanak's and Guru Gobind Singh's birthdays. In the gurdwaras the Guru Granth Sahib is read continuously and services are held. On these days street processions are also held. The Guru Granth Sahib is put on a decorated float, is headed by the panj piarey and followed by the congregation singing hymns. Free food is distributed to all passers-by.

Page 29 The family and the wider Sikh community share the responsibility for passing on the teachings of their religion to their young.

My name is
Simran Singh.
I am a Sikh
boy.

We Sikhs believe that there is only one God.

This symbol helps us to remember the one God.

God alone made this world
and everything in it.
God is everywhere and
always there for us.

God made all the people,
black and white.

Everyone is an equal member of
God's family and God loves us all.
We all pray to thank God.

Where do you pray?

Sikhs pray at the **gurdwara**.
The gurdwara can be a room
at home where the family pray.

It can also be a large building where many people meet to pray. This is the Golden Temple in India.

Our holy book is called the Guru Granth Sahib. It is kept in the main prayer hall. It rests on cushions and is covered in beautiful cloths.

What does Guru mean?

Guru means 'wise teacher'.
Guru Nanak was a wise teacher.
He started the Sikh religion.

Why is your hair so long?

Not cutting hair is part of the Sikh religion.

My mum ties my hair in a knot and covers it with a **patka**.

My dad covers his hair with a turban.
When we go to the gurdwara,
my mum wears a long scarf
called a chunni to cover her head.

Before we enter the gurdwara,
we take our shoes off and
cover our heads.

This shows respect to the
Guru Granth Sahib.

Then we sit down and listen
to the singing of hymns.
These hymns are called **shabads**.

The words are in **Panjabi**. They are
written in the Guru Granth Sahib.

There are special musicians who sing shabads in the gurdwara.

They play the **harmonium** and Indian drums called the **tabla**.

**Do only Sikhs pray
in the gurdwara?**

No, anyone who wants to pray to
God can join the prayers.

Men and women
share all the jobs
in the gurdwara.

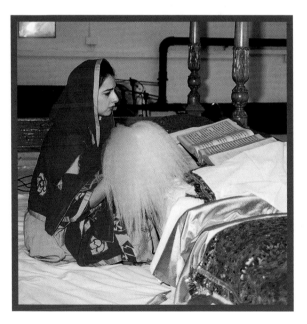

Women also lead
the services
and ceremonies.

After the service, everyone is given food called the **langar**.

We eat the langar in a large room at the gurdwara.

This eating together shows
we are all God's family.

What are you reading?

I am learning to read Panjabi, so that I can read the Guru Granth Sahib.

My aunty reads me stories
about the lives of our Gurus
and other famous Sikhs.

She also tells me about the Five Ks.

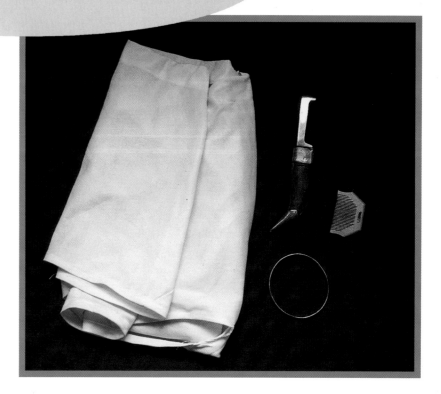

The five things that Sikhs wear.
In Panjabi they begin with the letter K.
Here are four of them.
The fifth is uncut hair.

What is your favourite time of year?

I like the Vaisakhi festival, on 14th of April. On this day long ago Sikhs were asked to wear the Five Ks.

We send cards and sweets to our friends to bless them and wish them a happy time. I give my pocket money to charity.

I tell my little brother about the special days and about the Gurus. I teach him how to be a good Sikh.

Glossary

gurdwara - a Sikh place of worship.

harmonium - an Indian musical instrument with a key board.

langar - Guru's kitchen; the gurdwara dining hall and the food served in it.

Panjabi - language spoken by Punjabis.

patka - a head covering used by boys before they start wearing a turban.

shabads - hymns from the Guru Granth Sahib.

tabla - Indian drums.

Index